50 Keto Desserts for Cravings

By: Kelly Johnson

Table of Contents

- Keto Chocolate Chip Cookies
- Almond Flour Brownies
- Keto Cheesecake
- Sugar-Free Chocolate Mousse
- Coconut Macaroons
- Keto Lemon Bars
- Chia Seed Pudding
- Keto Pumpkin Pie
- Chocolate Avocado Pudding
- Peanut Butter Cups
- Keto Snickerdoodles
- Sugar-Free Jello
- Keto Berry Crumble
- Low-Carb Tiramisu
- Keto Ice Cream
- Flourless Chocolate Cake
- Keto Pecan Pie
- Vanilla Mug Cake
- Keto Raspberry Cheesecake Fat Bombs
- Chocolate Coconut Fat Bombs
- Keto Strawberry Shortcake
- Peanut Butter Cheesecake
- Keto Almond Joy Bars
- Chocolate-Dipped Strawberries
- Keto Pumpkin Spice Muffins
- Coconut Cream Pie
- Chocolate Chip Zucchini Bread
- Keto Snickers Bar
- Low-Carb Fudge
- Keto Raspberry Mousse
- Sugar-Free Banana Bread
- Keto Chocolate Lava Cake
- Low-Carb Chocolate Pudding
- Almond Flour Cookies
- Keto Key Lime Pie
- Chocolate Hazelnut Spread

- Keto Peanut Butter Cookies
- Coconut Flour Cake
- Keto Chocolate Frosted Cupcakes
- Keto Apple Crisp
- Sugar-Free Chocolate Bark
- Keto Blueberry Muffins
- Low-Carb Red Velvet Cake
- Keto Chocolate Dipped Coconut Truffles
- Keto Maple Pecan Pie
- Lemon Coconut Bars
- Keto Mocha Cake
- Sugar-Free Caramel Sauce
- Keto Cinnamon Roll Muffins
- Dark Chocolate Almond Clusters

Keto Chocolate Chip Cookies

Ingredients:

- 2 cups almond flour
- 1/2 teaspoon baking soda
- 1/4 teaspoon salt
- 1/2 cup unsalted butter, softened
- 1/2 cup erythritol or your preferred low-carb sweetener
- 1 teaspoon vanilla extract
- 1 large egg
- 1/2 cup sugar-free chocolate chips

Instructions:

1. **Preheat the Oven:** Preheat your oven to 350°F (175°C) and line a baking sheet with parchment paper.
2. **Mix Dry Ingredients:** In a bowl, whisk together almond flour, baking soda, and salt. Set aside.
3. **Cream Butter and Sweetener:** In a separate bowl, cream the softened butter and erythritol together until light and fluffy. This should take about 2-3 minutes.
4. **Add Egg and Vanilla:** Beat in the egg and vanilla extract until well combined.
5. **Combine Mixtures:** Gradually add the dry ingredients to the wet ingredients, mixing until fully incorporated. Fold in the sugar-free chocolate chips.
6. **Shape Cookies:** Using a tablespoon, scoop the dough onto the prepared baking sheet, leaving some space between each cookie as they will spread slightly.
7. **Bake:** Bake in the preheated oven for 10-12 minutes or until the edges are golden brown. The centers may look slightly underbaked, but they will firm up as they cool.
8. **Cool:** Allow the cookies to cool on the baking sheet for 5 minutes before transferring them to a wire rack to cool completely.

Almond Flour Brownies

Ingredients:

- 1 cup almond flour
- ½ cup unsweetened cocoa powder
- ½ teaspoon baking powder
- ¼ teaspoon salt
- ½ cup melted butter (or coconut oil for dairy-free)
- ¾ cup sugar (or coconut sugar for a refined-sugar-free option)
- 2 large eggs
- 1 teaspoon vanilla extract
- ¼ cup dark chocolate chips (optional)
- ¼ cup chopped nuts (optional)

Instructions:

1. **Preheat the oven** to 350°F (175°C) and grease or line an 8x8-inch baking pan with parchment paper.
2. **Mix dry ingredients**: In a bowl, whisk together the almond flour, cocoa powder, baking powder, and salt.
3. **Combine wet ingredients**: In another bowl, whisk the melted butter, sugar, eggs, and vanilla until smooth.
4. **Combine wet and dry ingredients**: Gradually add the dry mixture into the wet mixture, stirring until well combined.
5. **Add mix-ins**: Fold in chocolate chips and nuts if desired.
6. **Bake**: Pour the batter into the prepared pan and spread evenly. Bake for 20-25 minutes, or until a toothpick inserted in the center comes out with a few moist crumbs.
7. **Cool and serve**: Let the brownies cool before slicing.

Keto Cheesecake

Ingredients:

- 1 ½ cups almond flour
- ½ cup unsweetened cocoa powder (for crust)
- ¼ cup erythritol or other keto-friendly sweetener
- ½ cup butter, melted
- 2 (8 oz) packages cream cheese, softened
- ¾ cup erythritol (for filling)
- 2 large eggs
- 1 teaspoon vanilla extract
- 1 tablespoon lemon juice

Instructions:

1. **Preheat the oven** to 325°F (160°C).
2. **Make the crust**: In a bowl, mix almond flour, cocoa powder, erythritol, and melted butter until crumbly. Press into the bottom of a 9-inch springform pan. Bake for 10 minutes.
3. **Prepare the filling**: In a large mixing bowl, beat the cream cheese and erythritol until smooth. Add eggs one at a time, mixing well after each. Stir in vanilla extract and lemon juice.
4. **Combine**: Pour the filling over the crust and smooth the top.
5. **Bake**: Bake for 45-50 minutes or until the center is set.
6. **Cool**: Let cool at room temperature, then refrigerate for at least 4 hours before serving.

Sugar-Free Chocolate Mousse

Ingredients:

- 1 cup heavy whipping cream
- ¼ cup unsweetened cocoa powder
- ¼ cup erythritol or other sugar substitute
- 1 teaspoon vanilla extract
- Pinch of salt

Instructions:

1. **Whip the cream**: In a mixing bowl, whip the heavy cream until soft peaks form.
2. **Add cocoa and sweetener**: Gently fold in the cocoa powder, erythritol, vanilla extract, and salt until well combined.
3. **Chill**: Spoon the mousse into serving dishes and refrigerate for at least 30 minutes before serving.

Coconut Macaroons

Ingredients:

- 2 ½ cups shredded unsweetened coconut
- ½ cup erythritol or other sugar substitute
- ¼ cup almond flour
- 3 large egg whites
- 1 teaspoon vanilla extract
- Pinch of salt

Instructions:

1. **Preheat the oven** to 325°F (160°C) and line a baking sheet with parchment paper.
2. **Mix ingredients**: In a bowl, combine shredded coconut, erythritol, almond flour, egg whites, vanilla extract, and salt until well mixed.
3. **Shape**: Use a scoop to form small mounds and place them on the prepared baking sheet.
4. **Bake**: Bake for 20-25 minutes or until the tops are golden brown.
5. **Cool**: Allow to cool on the baking sheet for a few minutes before transferring to a wire rack.

Keto Lemon Bars

Ingredients:

- **Crust:**
    - 1 ½ cups almond flour
    - ¼ cup erythritol or other keto-friendly sweetener
    - ½ cup unsalted butter, melted
- **Filling:**
    - 4 large eggs
    - ¾ cup erythritol
    - ½ cup fresh lemon juice
    - 2 teaspoons lemon zest
    - 1/4 teaspoon salt

Instructions:

1. **Preheat the oven** to 350°F (175°C) and grease an 8x8-inch baking dish.
2. **Make the crust**: In a bowl, combine almond flour, erythritol, and melted butter. Press into the bottom of the prepared dish. Bake for 10-12 minutes.
3. **Prepare the filling**: In another bowl, whisk together eggs, erythritol, lemon juice, lemon zest, and salt.
4. **Combine**: Pour the filling over the crust and bake for an additional 20-25 minutes, until set.
5. **Cool**: Allow to cool completely before slicing.

Chia Seed Pudding

Ingredients:

- 1/4 cup chia seeds
- 1 cup unsweetened almond milk
- 2 tablespoons erythritol or other sugar substitute
- 1 teaspoon vanilla extract

Instructions:

1. **Combine ingredients**: In a bowl, mix chia seeds, almond milk, erythritol, and vanilla extract.
2. **Mix well**: Stir thoroughly to prevent clumping.
3. **Refrigerate**: Cover and refrigerate for at least 4 hours or overnight until it thickens.
4. **Serve**: Stir again before serving and add toppings if desired.

Keto Pumpkin Pie

Ingredients:

- **Crust:**
    - 1 ½ cups almond flour
    - ¼ cup erythritol
    - ½ cup butter, melted
    - 1 large egg
- **Filling:**
    - 1 can (15 oz) pumpkin puree
    - ¾ cup erythritol
    - 2 large eggs
    - 1 teaspoon vanilla extract
    - 1 teaspoon cinnamon
    - ½ teaspoon nutmeg
    - ½ teaspoon ginger
    - ¼ teaspoon salt

Instructions:

1. **Preheat the oven** to 350°F (175°C).
2. **Make the crust**: In a bowl, mix almond flour, erythritol, melted butter, and egg until combined. Press into a pie dish. Bake for 10 minutes.
3. **Prepare the filling**: In a mixing bowl, combine pumpkin puree, erythritol, eggs, vanilla extract, spices, and salt.
4. **Combine**: Pour the filling into the crust and bake for 45-50 minutes, until set.
5. **Cool**: Allow to cool before slicing.

Chocolate Avocado Pudding

Ingredients:

- 2 ripe avocados
- 1/4 cup unsweetened cocoa powder
- 1/4 cup erythritol
- 1/2 cup almond milk
- 1 teaspoon vanilla extract

Instructions:

1. **Blend ingredients**: In a food processor, combine avocados, cocoa powder, erythritol, almond milk, and vanilla extract.
2. **Process until smooth**: Blend until creamy and smooth.
3. **Chill**: Spoon into serving dishes and refrigerate for at least 30 minutes before serving.

Peanut Butter Cups

Ingredients:

- 1 cup natural peanut butter
- 1/4 cup coconut oil
- 1/4 cup erythritol
- 1 cup sugar-free chocolate chips

Instructions:

1. **Prepare muffin tin**: Line a muffin tin with paper liners.
2. **Melt chocolate**: In a microwave-safe bowl, melt chocolate chips with coconut oil until smooth.
3. **Assemble cups**: Pour a small amount of chocolate into each liner, followed by a layer of peanut butter, and then top with more chocolate.
4. **Freeze**: Place in the freezer for about 30 minutes until set.

Keto Snickerdoodles

Ingredients:

- 2 cups almond flour
- 1/2 cup erythritol
- 1/2 teaspoon baking powder
- 1/4 teaspoon salt
- 1/2 teaspoon cinnamon
- 1/2 cup butter, softened
- 1 large egg

Instructions:

1. **Preheat the oven** to 350°F (175°C).
2. **Mix dry ingredients**: In a bowl, combine almond flour, erythritol, baking powder, salt, and cinnamon.
3. **Combine wet ingredients**: In another bowl, cream butter and egg until smooth.
4. **Combine mixtures**: Gradually add dry ingredients to wet ingredients until combined.
5. **Shape and bake**: Roll dough into balls, roll in cinnamon, and place on a baking sheet. Bake for 10-12 minutes.

Sugar-Free Jello

Ingredients:

- 1 cup boiling water
- 1 cup cold water
- 1 package sugar-free gelatin mix

Instructions:

1. **Dissolve gelatin**: In a bowl, dissolve gelatin in boiling water.
2. **Add cold water**: Stir in cold water and mix well.
3. **Refrigerate**: Pour into molds or cups and refrigerate until set, about 4 hours.

Keto Berry Crumble

Ingredients:

- **Filling:**
    - 2 cups mixed berries (fresh or frozen)
    - 2 tablespoons erythritol
- **Crumble topping:**
    - 1 cup almond flour
    - 1/4 cup coconut oil, melted
    - 1/4 cup erythritol
    - 1 teaspoon cinnamon

Instructions:

1. **Preheat the oven** to 350°F (175°C).
2. **Prepare filling**: In a bowl, combine berries and erythritol. Pour into a baking dish.
3. **Make crumble**: In another bowl, mix almond flour, coconut oil, erythritol, and cinnamon until crumbly.
4. **Assemble and bake**: Sprinkle crumble over the berries and bake for 25-30 minutes, until bubbly and golden.

Low-Carb Tiramisu

Ingredients:

- **Coffee Mixture:**
    - 1 cup brewed coffee, cooled
    - 1 tablespoon coffee liqueur (optional)
- **Mascarpone Filling:**
    - 1 cup mascarpone cheese
    - ½ cup heavy cream
    - ¼ cup erythritol
    - 1 teaspoon vanilla extract
- **Layering:**
    - 1 package low-carb ladyfingers (or sponge cake)
    - Cocoa powder for dusting

Instructions:

1. **Prepare coffee mixture**: In a bowl, combine brewed coffee and coffee liqueur (if using).
2. **Make mascarpone filling**: In another bowl, whip heavy cream until stiff peaks form. Fold in mascarpone cheese, erythritol, and vanilla extract until smooth.
3. **Assemble**: Dip ladyfingers briefly in the coffee mixture, then layer in a serving dish. Spread half of the mascarpone filling over the ladyfingers, repeat layers, and finish with the remaining filling.
4. **Chill**: Refrigerate for at least 4 hours or overnight. Dust with cocoa powder before serving.

Keto Ice Cream

Ingredients:

- 2 cups heavy cream
- 1 cup unsweetened almond milk
- ¾ cup erythritol
- 1 teaspoon vanilla extract
- Pinch of salt

Instructions:

1. **Combine ingredients**: In a bowl, whisk together heavy cream, almond milk, erythritol, vanilla extract, and salt until well mixed.
2. **Chill**: Refrigerate the mixture for at least 2 hours.
3. **Churn**: Pour into an ice cream maker and churn according to the manufacturer's instructions until creamy.
4. **Freeze**: Transfer to a container and freeze for a few hours before serving.

Flourless Chocolate Cake

Ingredients:

- 1 cup dark chocolate chips (sugar-free)
- ½ cup butter
- ¾ cup erythritol
- 3 large eggs
- 1 teaspoon vanilla extract
- ¼ cup unsweetened cocoa powder

Instructions:

1. **Preheat the oven** to 375°F (190°C) and grease a 9-inch round cake pan.
2. **Melt chocolate and butter**: In a microwave-safe bowl, melt chocolate chips and butter together until smooth.
3. **Combine ingredients**: Stir in erythritol, then add eggs one at a time, mixing well after each. Finally, stir in vanilla extract and cocoa powder.
4. **Bake**: Pour the batter into the prepared pan and bake for 20-25 minutes. Let cool before serving.

Keto Pecan Pie

Ingredients:

- **Crust:**
    - 1 ½ cups almond flour
    - ¼ cup butter, melted
    - ¼ cup erythritol
- **Filling:**
    - 2 cups pecans, chopped
    - 3 large eggs
    - 1 cup sugar-free syrup (like Lakanto or monk fruit)
    - 1 teaspoon vanilla extract
    - ½ teaspoon salt

Instructions:

1. **Preheat the oven** to 350°F (175°C).
2. **Make the crust**: In a bowl, mix almond flour, melted butter, and erythritol until crumbly. Press into a pie dish. Bake for 10 minutes.
3. **Prepare filling**: In another bowl, whisk together eggs, sugar-free syrup, vanilla extract, and salt. Stir in chopped pecans.
4. **Assemble**: Pour the filling into the crust and bake for 35-40 minutes, until set.
5. **Cool**: Allow to cool before slicing.

Vanilla Mug Cake

Ingredients:

- 4 tablespoons almond flour
- 1 tablespoon erythritol
- ½ teaspoon baking powder
- 1 large egg
- 1 tablespoon unsweetened almond milk
- 1 tablespoon butter, melted
- ½ teaspoon vanilla extract

Instructions:

1. **Combine dry ingredients**: In a microwave-safe mug, mix almond flour, erythritol, and baking powder.
2. **Add wet ingredients**: Add the egg, almond milk, melted butter, and vanilla extract. Stir until well combined.
3. **Microwave**: Microwave on high for 60-90 seconds, until the cake is set. Let cool slightly before enjoying.

Keto Raspberry Cheesecake Fat Bombs

Ingredients:

- 1 cup cream cheese, softened
- ½ cup unsweetened almond butter
- ½ cup erythritol
- ½ cup fresh raspberries (or raspberry extract)
- 1 teaspoon vanilla extract

Instructions:

1. **Blend ingredients**: In a bowl, combine cream cheese, almond butter, erythritol, raspberries, and vanilla extract until smooth.
2. **Scoop**: Spoon the mixture into silicone molds or mini muffin tins.
3. **Freeze**: Freeze for 1-2 hours until solid. Pop out and store in the freezer.

Chocolate Coconut Fat Bombs

Ingredients:

- 1 cup coconut oil, melted
- ½ cup unsweetened cocoa powder
- ½ cup erythritol
- 1 teaspoon vanilla extract

Instructions:

1. **Mix ingredients**: In a bowl, combine melted coconut oil, cocoa powder, erythritol, and vanilla extract until smooth.
2. **Pour into molds**: Spoon the mixture into silicone molds or mini muffin tins.
3. **Freeze**: Freeze until solid, about 1-2 hours. Store in the freezer.

Keto Strawberry Shortcake

Ingredients:

- **Cake:**
    - 1 ½ cups almond flour
    - ½ cup erythritol
    - ½ teaspoon baking powder
    - 3 large eggs
    - ½ cup unsweetened almond milk
    - ¼ cup melted butter
- **Topping:**
    - 1 cup heavy whipping cream
    - 2 tablespoons erythritol
    - 1 cup strawberries, sliced

Instructions:

1. **Preheat the oven** to 350°F (175°C) and grease an 8-inch round cake pan.
2. **Mix dry ingredients**: In a bowl, combine almond flour, erythritol, and baking powder.
3. **Combine wet ingredients**: In another bowl, whisk together eggs, almond milk, and melted butter.
4. **Combine mixtures**: Gradually add the dry ingredients to the wet ingredients until well combined.
5. **Bake**: Pour the batter into the prepared pan and bake for 25-30 minutes, until a toothpick comes out clean.
6. **Whip cream**: In a separate bowl, whip heavy cream with erythritol until soft peaks form.
7. **Assemble**: Once the cake is cool, slice it and layer with whipped cream and strawberries.

Peanut Butter Cheesecake

Ingredients:

- **Crust:**
    - 1 ½ cups almond flour
    - ½ cup erythritol
    - ½ cup butter, melted
- **Filling:**
    - 16 oz cream cheese, softened
    - 1 cup natural peanut butter
    - ½ cup erythritol
    - 3 large eggs
    - 1 teaspoon vanilla extract

Instructions:

1. **Preheat the oven** to 350°F (175°C) and grease a 9-inch springform pan.
2. **Make the crust**: In a bowl, mix almond flour, erythritol, and melted butter until crumbly. Press into the bottom of the springform pan.
3. **Prepare the filling**: In a large bowl, beat together cream cheese, peanut butter, erythritol, eggs, and vanilla extract until smooth and creamy.
4. **Assemble**: Pour the filling over the crust and smooth the top.
5. **Bake**: Bake for 40-45 minutes until set. Allow to cool before refrigerating for at least 4 hours before serving.

Keto Almond Joy Bars

Ingredients:

- **Base Layer:**
    - 1 cup almond flour
    - ¼ cup cocoa powder
    - ½ cup unsweetened shredded coconut
    - ½ cup erythritol
    - ½ cup melted coconut oil
- **Filling:**
    - 1 cup almond butter
    - ¼ cup erythritol
    - ½ teaspoon vanilla extract
- **Chocolate Topping:**
    - 1 cup sugar-free dark chocolate chips
    - 2 tablespoons coconut oil

Instructions:

1. **Prepare the base**: In a bowl, combine almond flour, cocoa powder, shredded coconut, erythritol, and melted coconut oil until well mixed. Press the mixture into the bottom of a lined 8x8 inch baking dish.
2. **Make the filling**: In a separate bowl, mix almond butter, erythritol, and vanilla extract until smooth. Spread the filling over the base layer.
3. **Prepare the topping**: In a microwave-safe bowl, melt dark chocolate chips with coconut oil. Stir until smooth, then pour over the filling.
4. **Chill**: Refrigerate until set, about 2 hours. Cut into bars and serve.

Chocolate-Dipped Strawberries

Ingredients:

- 1 cup fresh strawberries, washed and dried
- ½ cup sugar-free dark chocolate chips
- 1 tablespoon coconut oil

Instructions:

1. **Melt chocolate**: In a microwave-safe bowl, combine chocolate chips and coconut oil. Microwave in 30-second intervals, stirring in between until fully melted.
2. **Dip strawberries**: Dip each strawberry into the melted chocolate, allowing excess to drip off.
3. **Set**: Place dipped strawberries on a parchment-lined baking sheet. Refrigerate until the chocolate hardens.

Keto Pumpkin Spice Muffins

Ingredients:

- 1 ½ cups almond flour
- ½ cup erythritol
- 1 teaspoon baking powder
- 1 teaspoon pumpkin pie spice
- ½ teaspoon salt
- 3 large eggs
- 1 cup canned pumpkin puree
- ¼ cup melted coconut oil

Instructions:

1. **Preheat the oven** to 350°F (175°C) and line a muffin tin with liners.
2. **Combine dry ingredients**: In a bowl, mix almond flour, erythritol, baking powder, pumpkin pie spice, and salt.
3. **Combine wet ingredients**: In another bowl, whisk together eggs, pumpkin puree, and melted coconut oil.
4. **Mix together**: Add the wet ingredients to the dry ingredients and stir until well combined.
5. **Bake**: Fill muffin cups about ¾ full and bake for 20-25 minutes, until a toothpick comes out clean.

Coconut Cream Pie

Ingredients:

- **Crust:**
    - 1 ½ cups almond flour
    - ¼ cup erythritol
    - ½ cup butter, melted
- **Filling:**
    - 1 cup coconut cream
    - ½ cup unsweetened shredded coconut
    - ½ cup erythritol
    - 1 teaspoon vanilla extract
    - 3 large eggs
- **Topping:**
    - 1 cup heavy whipping cream
    - 2 tablespoons erythritol

Instructions:

1. **Preheat the oven** to 350°F (175°C) and grease a pie dish.
2. **Make the crust**: In a bowl, combine almond flour, erythritol, and melted butter. Press into the bottom and up the sides of the pie dish. Bake for 10 minutes.
3. **Prepare the filling**: In a bowl, mix coconut cream, shredded coconut, erythritol, vanilla extract, and eggs until smooth.
4. **Assemble**: Pour the filling into the baked crust and bake for 25-30 minutes until set.
5. **Chill**: Allow to cool, then refrigerate for at least 2 hours.
6. **Whip cream**: In a separate bowl, whip heavy cream with erythritol until soft peaks form. Spread over the cooled pie before serving.

Chocolate Chip Zucchini Bread

Ingredients:

- 2 cups almond flour
- ½ cup erythritol
- 1 teaspoon baking soda
- ½ teaspoon baking powder
- ½ teaspoon salt
- 1 teaspoon cinnamon
- 3 large eggs
- 1 cup grated zucchini (squeezed dry)
- ½ cup sugar-free chocolate chips

Instructions:

1. **Preheat the oven** to 350°F (175°C) and grease a loaf pan.
2. **Mix dry ingredients**: In a bowl, combine almond flour, erythritol, baking soda, baking powder, salt, and cinnamon.
3. **Combine wet ingredients**: In another bowl, whisk together eggs and grated zucchini.
4. **Combine mixtures**: Add the wet ingredients to the dry ingredients and stir until well combined. Fold in chocolate chips.
5. **Bake**: Pour the batter into the prepared loaf pan and bake for 45-50 minutes, until a toothpick comes out clean.

Keto Snickers Bar

Ingredients:

- **Base Layer:**
    - 1 cup almond flour
    - ¼ cup cocoa powder
    - ¼ cup erythritol
    - ½ cup butter, melted
- **Caramel Layer:**
    - ½ cup sugar-free peanut butter
    - ¼ cup erythritol
    - ½ cup unsweetened coconut milk
- **Chocolate Topping:**
    - 1 cup sugar-free dark chocolate chips
    - 2 tablespoons coconut oil

Instructions:

1. **Prepare the base**: In a bowl, mix almond flour, cocoa powder, erythritol, and melted butter until combined. Press into a lined 8x8 inch baking dish.
2. **Make the caramel**: In a saucepan over low heat, combine peanut butter, erythritol, and coconut milk. Stir until smooth. Spread the caramel over the base layer.
3. **Prepare the topping**: Melt chocolate chips with coconut oil in a microwave-safe bowl. Stir until smooth, then pour over the caramel layer.
4. **Chill**: Refrigerate until set, about 2 hours. Cut into bars and serve.

Low-Carb Fudge

Ingredients:

- ½ cup coconut oil
- ½ cup unsweetened cocoa powder
- ½ cup erythritol
- 1 teaspoon vanilla extract
- Pinch of salt

Instructions:

1. **Melt ingredients**: In a saucepan over low heat, melt coconut oil.
2. **Combine**: Stir in cocoa powder, erythritol, vanilla extract, and salt until smooth.
3. **Pour**: Pour the mixture into a lined 8x8 inch baking dish.
4. **Chill**: Refrigerate until firm, about 2 hours. Cut into squares and serve.

Keto Raspberry Mousse

Ingredients:

- 1 cup fresh raspberries
- 1 cup heavy whipping cream
- ¼ cup erythritol
- 1 teaspoon vanilla extract
- Pinch of salt

Instructions:

1. **Puree raspberries**: In a blender, puree the raspberries until smooth. Strain through a fine mesh sieve to remove seeds if desired.
2. **Whip cream**: In a bowl, whip the heavy cream until soft peaks form.
3. **Combine**: Gently fold in the raspberry puree, erythritol, vanilla extract, and salt until combined.
4. **Chill**: Spoon the mousse into serving dishes and refrigerate for at least 2 hours before serving.

Sugar-Free Banana Bread

Ingredients:

- 2 cups almond flour
- ½ cup erythritol
- 2 large eggs
- 1 cup ripe bananas, mashed (about 2 bananas)
- 1 teaspoon baking powder
- 1 teaspoon vanilla extract
- ½ teaspoon cinnamon
- ½ teaspoon salt

Instructions:

1. **Preheat the oven** to 350°F (175°C) and grease a loaf pan.
2. **Mix dry ingredients**: In a bowl, combine almond flour, erythritol, baking powder, cinnamon, and salt.
3. **Combine wet ingredients**: In another bowl, mix eggs, mashed bananas, and vanilla extract.
4. **Combine mixtures**: Add the wet ingredients to the dry ingredients and stir until well combined.
5. **Bake**: Pour the batter into the prepared loaf pan and bake for 30-35 minutes, until a toothpick comes out clean.

Keto Chocolate Lava Cake

Ingredients:

- ½ cup unsweetened chocolate, chopped
- ½ cup butter
- ¾ cup erythritol
- 2 large eggs
- 2 egg yolks
- 1 teaspoon vanilla extract
- ¼ cup almond flour

Instructions:

1. **Preheat the oven** to 425°F (220°C) and grease four ramekins.
2. **Melt chocolate and butter**: In a saucepan over low heat, melt the chocolate and butter until smooth.
3. **Mix ingredients**: In a bowl, whisk together erythritol, eggs, egg yolks, and vanilla extract. Stir in the melted chocolate mixture and almond flour until combined.
4. **Bake**: Divide the batter among the ramekins and bake for 12-14 minutes until the edges are set but the center is soft.
5. **Serve**: Let cool for 1 minute, then invert onto plates and serve warm.

Low-Carb Chocolate Pudding

Ingredients:

- 2 cups unsweetened almond milk
- ¼ cup erythritol
- ½ cup unsweetened cocoa powder
- 2 tablespoons cornstarch or keto-friendly thickener
- 1 teaspoon vanilla extract
- Pinch of salt

Instructions:

1. **Combine dry ingredients**: In a saucepan, whisk together erythritol, cocoa powder, cornstarch, and salt.
2. **Add milk**: Gradually add almond milk, whisking until smooth.
3. **Cook**: Place over medium heat and cook, stirring constantly until the mixture thickens, about 5-7 minutes.
4. **Cool**: Remove from heat and stir in vanilla extract. Let cool, then refrigerate until set.

Almond Flour Cookies

Ingredients:

- 2 cups almond flour
- ½ cup erythritol
- 1 large egg
- ½ teaspoon baking powder
- 1 teaspoon vanilla extract
- Pinch of salt

Instructions:

1. **Preheat the oven** to 350°F (175°C) and line a baking sheet with parchment paper.
2. **Mix ingredients**: In a bowl, combine almond flour, erythritol, egg, baking powder, vanilla extract, and salt until a dough forms.
3. **Shape cookies**: Scoop tablespoon-sized portions onto the baking sheet, flattening slightly.
4. **Bake**: Bake for 10-12 minutes until edges are golden. Let cool before serving.

Keto Key Lime Pie

Ingredients:

- **Crust:**
    - 1 ½ cups almond flour
    - ¼ cup erythritol
    - ½ cup butter, melted
- **Filling:**
    - 3 large eggs
    - 1 cup erythritol
    - ½ cup fresh lime juice
    - Zest of 2 limes
    - 1 cup heavy cream

Instructions:

1. **Preheat the oven** to 350°F (175°C) and grease a pie dish.
2. **Make the crust**: In a bowl, mix almond flour, erythritol, and melted butter until crumbly. Press into the bottom and up the sides of the pie dish. Bake for 10 minutes.
3. **Prepare the filling**: In a bowl, whisk together eggs, erythritol, lime juice, and lime zest.
4. **Assemble**: Pour the filling into the baked crust.
5. **Bake**: Bake for 25-30 minutes until set. Cool and refrigerate before serving.
6. **Whip cream**: Optional: Whip heavy cream and top the pie before serving.

Chocolate Hazelnut Spread

Ingredients:

- 1 cup hazelnuts, toasted
- ¼ cup cocoa powder
- ½ cup erythritol
- 2 tablespoons coconut oil
- 1 teaspoon vanilla extract
- Pinch of salt

Instructions:

1. **Blend hazelnuts**: In a food processor, blend toasted hazelnuts until smooth.
2. **Add ingredients**: Add cocoa powder, erythritol, coconut oil, vanilla extract, and salt. Blend until creamy and well combined.
3. **Store**: Transfer to a jar and store in the refrigerator.

Keto Peanut Butter Cookies

Ingredients:

- 1 cup natural peanut butter
- ½ cup erythritol
- 1 large egg
- 1 teaspoon vanilla extract

Instructions:

1. **Preheat the oven** to 350°F (175°C) and line a baking sheet with parchment paper.
2. **Mix ingredients**: In a bowl, combine peanut butter, erythritol, egg, and vanilla extract until well mixed.
3. **Shape cookies**: Scoop tablespoon-sized portions onto the baking sheet, flattening slightly with a fork.
4. **Bake**: Bake for 10-12 minutes until set. Let cool before serving.

Coconut Flour Cake

Ingredients:

- ½ cup coconut flour
- ½ cup erythritol
- ½ cup unsweetened applesauce
- 4 large eggs
- ½ cup coconut oil, melted
- 1 teaspoon baking powder
- 1 teaspoon vanilla extract
- Pinch of salt

Instructions:

1. **Preheat the oven** to 350°F (175°C) and grease an 8-inch cake pan.
2. **Mix dry ingredients**: In a bowl, combine coconut flour, erythritol, baking powder, and salt.
3. **Combine wet ingredients**: In another bowl, whisk together eggs, applesauce, melted coconut oil, and vanilla extract.
4. **Combine mixtures**: Add the wet ingredients to the dry ingredients and stir until well combined.
5. **Bake**: Pour the batter into the prepared pan and bake for 25-30 minutes, until a toothpick comes out clean.

Keto Chocolate Frosted Cupcakes

Ingredients:

- **Cupcakes:**
    - 1 cup almond flour
    - ¼ cup unsweetened cocoa powder
    - ½ cup erythritol
    - 4 large eggs
    - ½ cup butter, melted
    - 1 teaspoon baking powder
    - 1 teaspoon vanilla extract
- **Frosting:**
    - ½ cup unsweetened cocoa powder
    - ½ cup butter, softened
    - ½ cup erythritol
    - 2 tablespoons heavy cream
    - 1 teaspoon vanilla extract

Instructions:

1. **Preheat the oven** to 350°F (175°C) and line a muffin tin with cupcake liners.
2. **Make cupcakes**: In a bowl, combine almond flour, cocoa powder, erythritol, baking powder, eggs, melted butter, and vanilla extract. Mix until smooth.
3. **Bake**: Divide the batter among the cupcake liners and bake for 18-20 minutes, until a toothpick comes out clean.
4. **Make frosting**: In a separate bowl, beat together cocoa powder, softened butter, erythritol, heavy cream, and vanilla extract until creamy.
5. **Frost cupcakes**: Once the cupcakes have cooled, frost with the chocolate frosting.

Keto Apple Crisp

Ingredients:

- **Filling:**
    - 3 cups peeled and sliced apples (use a keto-friendly variety)
    - ½ cup erythritol
    - 1 teaspoon cinnamon
- **Topping:**
    - 1 cup almond flour
    - ½ cup rolled oats (or substitute with more almond flour)
    - ¼ cup butter, melted
    - ¼ cup erythritol
    - 1 teaspoon vanilla extract

Instructions:

1. **Preheat the oven** to 350°F (175°C).
2. **Prepare filling**: In a bowl, mix the sliced apples, erythritol, and cinnamon. Spread the mixture in a baking dish.
3. **Prepare topping**: In another bowl, combine almond flour, oats, melted butter, erythritol, and vanilla extract until crumbly.
4. **Assemble**: Sprinkle the topping over the apple filling.
5. **Bake**: Bake for 30-35 minutes until the apples are tender and the topping is golden.

Sugar-Free Chocolate Bark

Ingredients:

- 1 cup sugar-free chocolate chips
- ½ cup nuts (e.g., almonds, walnuts, pecans)
- ¼ cup dried unsweetened coconut flakes
- Sea salt (optional)

Instructions:

1. **Melt chocolate**: In a microwave or double boiler, melt the sugar-free chocolate chips until smooth.
2. **Add toppings**: Stir in the nuts and coconut flakes.
3. **Spread**: Pour the mixture onto a parchment-lined baking sheet and spread evenly.
4. **Chill**: Refrigerate until set, about 1 hour.
5. **Break into pieces**: Once hardened, break the chocolate bark into pieces.

Keto Blueberry Muffins

Ingredients:

- 1 ½ cups almond flour
- ½ cup erythritol
- ½ teaspoon baking powder
- ½ teaspoon baking soda
- ½ teaspoon salt
- 3 large eggs
- ½ cup unsweetened almond milk
- 1 teaspoon vanilla extract
- 1 cup fresh blueberries

Instructions:

1. **Preheat the oven** to 350°F (175°C) and line a muffin tin with liners.
2. **Mix dry ingredients**: In a bowl, combine almond flour, erythritol, baking powder, baking soda, and salt.
3. **Combine wet ingredients**: In another bowl, whisk together eggs, almond milk, and vanilla extract.
4. **Combine mixtures**: Add the wet ingredients to the dry ingredients and fold in the blueberries.
5. **Bake**: Divide the batter among the muffin cups and bake for 18-20 minutes, until a toothpick comes out clean.

Low-Carb Red Velvet Cake

Ingredients:

- 1 ½ cups almond flour
- ¼ cup cocoa powder
- ¾ cup erythritol
- ½ cup butter, softened
- 3 large eggs
- 1 teaspoon vanilla extract
- 1 teaspoon baking powder
- 1 teaspoon red food coloring
- Pinch of salt

Instructions:

1. **Preheat the oven** to 350°F (175°C) and grease a round cake pan.
2. **Mix dry ingredients**: In a bowl, combine almond flour, cocoa powder, erythritol, baking powder, and salt.
3. **Combine wet ingredients**: In another bowl, cream the softened butter and erythritol together. Add eggs, vanilla extract, and red food coloring, mixing until smooth.
4. **Combine mixtures**: Add the dry ingredients to the wet ingredients and mix until well combined.
5. **Bake**: Pour the batter into the prepared pan and bake for 25-30 minutes, until a toothpick comes out clean.

Keto Chocolate Dipped Coconut Truffles

Ingredients:

- 1 cup unsweetened shredded coconut
- ½ cup coconut cream
- ¼ cup erythritol
- 1 teaspoon vanilla extract
- 1 cup sugar-free chocolate chips

Instructions:

1. **Mix ingredients**: In a bowl, combine shredded coconut, coconut cream, erythritol, and vanilla extract until well combined.
2. **Form truffles**: Roll the mixture into small balls and place them on a parchment-lined tray.
3. **Chill**: Refrigerate the truffles for 30 minutes until firm.
4. **Melt chocolate**: In a microwave or double boiler, melt the sugar-free chocolate chips.
5. **Dip truffles**: Dip each truffle into the melted chocolate and return to the tray.
6. **Chill again**: Refrigerate until the chocolate has set.

Keto Maple Pecan Pie

Ingredients:

- **Crust:**
    - 1 ½ cups almond flour
    - ¼ cup erythritol
    - ½ cup butter, melted
- **Filling:**
    - 1 cup pecans, chopped
    - ½ cup erythritol
    - ½ cup unsweetened almond milk
    - ¼ cup sugar-free maple syrup
    - 3 large eggs
    - 1 teaspoon vanilla extract
    - 1 teaspoon cinnamon

Instructions:

1. **Preheat the oven** to 350°F (175°C) and grease a pie dish.
2. **Make the crust**: In a bowl, mix almond flour, erythritol, and melted butter until crumbly. Press into the bottom and sides of the pie dish.
3. **Prepare the filling**: In a separate bowl, mix pecans, erythritol, almond milk, maple syrup, eggs, vanilla extract, and cinnamon until combined.
4. **Assemble**: Pour the filling into the prepared crust.
5. **Bake**: Bake for 30-35 minutes until the filling is set. Let cool before serving.

Lemon Coconut Bars

Ingredients:

- **Crust:**
    - 1 ½ cups almond flour
    - ¼ cup erythritol
    - ½ cup melted butter
- **Filling:**
    - 1 cup unsweetened shredded coconut
    - ½ cup lemon juice
    - ½ cup erythritol
    - 3 large eggs
    - 1 teaspoon vanilla extract

Instructions:

1. **Preheat the oven** to 350°F (175°C) and grease an 8x8-inch baking dish.
2. **Make the crust**: In a bowl, mix almond flour, erythritol, and melted butter until crumbly. Press the mixture into the bottom of the baking dish.
3. **Bake the crust**: Bake for 10-12 minutes until lightly golden.
4. **Prepare the filling**: In another bowl, whisk together shredded coconut, lemon juice, erythritol, eggs, and vanilla extract until well combined.
5. **Assemble**: Pour the filling over the baked crust.
6. **Bake**: Bake for an additional 20-25 minutes, until the filling is set. Let cool before slicing into bars.

Keto Mocha Cake

Ingredients:

- 1 cup almond flour
- ¼ cup unsweetened cocoa powder
- ½ cup erythritol
- 4 large eggs
- ½ cup brewed coffee, cooled
- ½ cup melted butter
- 1 teaspoon baking powder
- 1 teaspoon vanilla extract

Instructions:

1. **Preheat the oven** to 350°F (175°C) and grease an 8-inch round cake pan.
2. **Mix dry ingredients**: In a bowl, combine almond flour, cocoa powder, erythritol, and baking powder.
3. **Combine wet ingredients**: In another bowl, whisk together eggs, brewed coffee, melted butter, and vanilla extract.
4. **Combine mixtures**: Add the wet ingredients to the dry ingredients and mix until smooth.
5. **Bake**: Pour the batter into the prepared cake pan and bake for 25-30 minutes, until a toothpick comes out clean.

Sugar-Free Caramel Sauce

Ingredients:

- ½ cup unsalted butter
- ½ cup erythritol
- ¼ cup heavy cream
- 1 teaspoon vanilla extract
- Pinch of salt

Instructions:

1. **Melt butter**: In a saucepan over medium heat, melt the butter.
2. **Add erythritol**: Stir in erythritol and bring to a gentle simmer.
3. **Add cream**: Slowly whisk in the heavy cream and cook for an additional 2-3 minutes until thickened.
4. **Finish**: Remove from heat, then stir in vanilla extract and salt. Let cool before using.

Keto Cinnamon Roll Muffins

Ingredients:

- **Muffins:**
    - 2 cups almond flour
    - ¼ cup erythritol
    - 2 large eggs
    - ½ cup unsweetened almond milk
    - 1 teaspoon baking powder
    - 1 teaspoon cinnamon
- **Filling:**
    - ¼ cup erythritol
    - 2 tablespoons cinnamon
    - ¼ cup butter, melted

Instructions:

1. **Preheat the oven** to 350°F (175°C) and line a muffin tin with liners.
2. **Mix dry ingredients**: In a bowl, combine almond flour, erythritol, baking powder, and cinnamon.
3. **Combine wet ingredients**: In another bowl, whisk together eggs and almond milk.
4. **Combine mixtures**: Add the wet ingredients to the dry ingredients and mix until combined.
5. **Prepare filling**: In a separate bowl, mix erythritol, cinnamon, and melted butter.
6. **Assemble**: Divide half the muffin batter among the liners, add a spoonful of filling, then top with remaining batter.
7. **Bake**: Bake for 18-20 minutes, until a toothpick comes out clean.

Dark Chocolate Almond Clusters

Ingredients:

- 1 cup almonds, whole or sliced
- 1 cup sugar-free dark chocolate chips
- Sea salt (optional)

Instructions:

1. **Melt chocolate**: In a microwave or double boiler, melt the sugar-free dark chocolate chips until smooth.
2. **Mix almonds**: Stir in the almonds until they are fully coated with chocolate.
3. **Form clusters**: Drop spoonfuls of the mixture onto a parchment-lined baking sheet, forming clusters.
4. **Chill**: Refrigerate until set, about 30 minutes.
5. **Finish**: Sprinkle with sea salt if desired before serving.

www.ingramcontent.com/pod-product-compliance
Lightning Source LLC
LaVergne TN
LVHW081340060526
838201LV00055B/2766